Still a Chance to Learn?

Report of a project funded by the Joseph Rowntree Foundation on the Further and Higher Education Act (1992) and adults with learning difficulties

Margaret Macadam,
Norah Fry Research Centre, University of Bristol

Jeannie Sutcliffe,
National Institute of Adult Continuing Education

The **Joseph Rowntree Foundation** has supported this project as part of its programme of research and innovative development projects, which it hopes will be of value to policy makers and practitioners. The facts presented and views expressed in this report, however, are those of the authors and not necessarily those of the Foundation.

Published by the National Institute of Adult Continuing Education (England and Wales)
21 De Montfort Street, Leicester LE1 7GE

Company registration no. 2603322
Charity registration no. 1002775

First published 1996

Cataloguing in Publication Data
A CIP record for this title is available from the British Library

ISBN 1 872941 99 0

Printed in Great Britain by
Wilton, Wright & Son Ltd., Surrey

Contents

Acknowledgements

We would like to thank the following for their help, support and enthusiasm:

> All the people in colleges and LEAs who helped by filling in our questionnaire. The survey could not have been done without you! Special thanks also to all those who gave their time to be interviewed for the project.

> All the people in self advocacy groups who replied to our tape and letter.

> Lesley Jones and Linda Ward from the Joseph Rowntree Foundation.

> Anne Agius and Maggi Walton, who both gave invaluable secretarial support.

> Ruth Townsley, who undertook the site visit interviews.

Members of the Research Advisory Group

Jacqui Buffton, Gloucestershire County Council
Margaret Flynn, National Development Team
Joan Giles, OFSTED
Pat Hood, Adviser to the Further Education Funding
      Council's learning difficulties and/or disabilities
      committee
Christopher Johns, Social Services Inspectorate
John Lawton, Mencap
Christopher Lock, Consultant, Community Care Services
Alyson Malach, City of Liverpool Community College
David Swindells, University of Huddersfield

Members of the advisory group of students with learning difficulties and supporters

Woodspring People First

Susan Iles
Debbie Lewis
Jeremy Wells

Supporters:

Linda Oldham
Sue Hogarth
Anne Kilpin

South Bristol College

Tiffany England
Neil Palmer
Brian Vasey

Supporter:

Val Williams

Last, but not least, many thanks to Ken Simons for writing the original project bid to obtain funding for the work.

1:
Introduction

Why was this research undertaken?

The Further and Higher Education Act (1992) introduced great changes to the way in which continuing education is delivered in colleges and local education authorities across England and Wales. The *Still a Chance to Learn?* project set out to explore the impact of these changes specifically on education for adults with learning difficulties.

The National Institute of Adult Continuing Education (NIACE) has a track record in documenting good practice in the education of adults with learning difficulties, much of it with backing from the Joseph Rowntree Foundation.[1] In *Still a Chance to Learn?* we wanted to explore whether the sorts of innovatory practice we had written about before were still possible under the new system, and to explore the implications of the Act by asking college and LEA staff about changes in their provision as a result of the legislation. The views of adults with learning difficulties were also sought as an important focus of the work. The project was a collaboration between NIACE and the Norah Fry Research Centre at the University of Bristol, and was supported by the Joseph Rowntree Foundation.

A word about terminology

In the legal terminology of the Further and Higher Education Act, the term learning difficulties is used in a wide ranging way to refer to people with **all** sorts of learning difficulties and disabilities. However, this research

---

[1] NIACE has published four good practice handbooks and two staff development packs on education for adults with learning difficulties: see references section on pages 15/16 for details.

covered education in colleges and LEAs only for adults with:

- severe learning difficulties
- moderate learning difficulties
- profound/complex learning difficulties, where students have an additional disability as well as learning difficulties.

The research did not cover people with other disabilities or mental health difficulties. Nor did it cover the full range of what used to be called 'special needs' provision, which sometimes covered basic skills and English for Speakers of Second Languages for all students as well as a wide range of classes for people with various disabilities.

We have used the term 'learning difficulties' for several important reasons. The majority of people described as having 'learning difficulties' prefer this term to the old fashioned and now out of date label 'mental handicap', or even the more recent term 'learning disability'. Research by Simons[2] has confirmed this preference. 'Learning difficulties' is the term favoured by many staff working with this group of students and is also used by the Further Education Funding Council.

Welcome mentions of adults with learning difficulties in the FHE Act legislation and circulars

Before the Further and Higher Education Act (1992), education for adults with learning difficulties was patchy in terms of both quality and quantity.[3] Some adults could attend college full-time, whereas some school leavers or older adults had nothing on offer to them. There was considerable scope for development. The Further and Higher Education Act (1992) caused a major restructuring of the way that adult and continuing education is organised and funded. The Act set out responsibility for the then

---

[2] See Simons K., (1993) *Sticking Up for Ourselves*, Joseph Rowntree Foundation
[3] See Sutcliffe J., (1990) *Adults with Learning Difficulties*, NIACE.

newly formed Further Education Funding Councils (FEFCs) to 'have regard' to the requirements of people with learning difficulties and disabilities. Local Education Authorities already had this responsibility. The Act also gave the FEFC a duty to secure provision outside the further education sector for education up to the age of 25 for adults with learning difficulties where appropriate. This legislation thus recognised the importance of an extended education for disabled people. There was also a recognition that education for people with learning difficulties was important to resource properly, as FEFC Circular 92/08 described: 'Some types of education, including education for students with learning difficulties, may be necessarily more expensive than others.' The FEFC demonstrated a clear commitment to education for people with learning difficulties and disabilities by setting up the Tomlinson Committee to review provision and make recommendations for the future. This three year committee of enquiry is due to report in 1996.

What concerns were there before the Further and Higher Education Act was implemented?

There were concerns about the impact of the Further and Higher Education Act on vulnerable groups. For example, after a major debate in the House of Lords, the FHE Act was amended to ensure that courses on independent living and communication skills were eligible for funding from the newly created funding councils. While some hoped that the FHE Act would provide new and improved opportunities for the inclusion of vulnerable minorities in mainstream adult and continuing education, others feared that some aspects might prove to be a step backwards.

Concerns expressed prior to the implementation of the Further and Higher Education Act included the possibility of restricted access due to a new emphasis on qualifications; the loss of key co-ordinating posts in Local Education

Authorities and fear of losing funding and provision.[4] The Act was meant to ensure that provision was not lost, with LEAs and colleges providing a seamless service. As one FEFC circular put it: 'The Further and Higher Education Act is designed to ensure that the existing range of further education provision for students with learning difficulties and disabilities is maintained.'[5] However, some professionals feared that the 'seamless service' would be hard to achieve in practice and that provision would be lost.

Timing of the research

The research outlined in this book took place in 1995, two years after the Further and Higher Education Act was implemented in April 1993. The effects of the legislation had therefore largely settled down after the initial implementation phase and it was an opportune time to review how the Act was working in practice and whether the early hopes and concerns expressed by professionals had been realised.

What main changes did the Further and Higher Education Act (1992) bring in for adults with learning difficulties?

Prior to the implementation of the Further and Higher Education Act (1992) in April 1993, funding was largely administered by Local Education Authorities in England and Wales, with some funding coming also from Training and Enterprise Councils, joint funding and voluntary organisations. The LEAs played a key role in funding provision regardless of whether courses took place at an adult education centre or at a further education college. The Further and Higher Education Act (1992) gave colleges independence from local authority control. Two Further Education Funding Councils were set up, one each in

---

[4] See articles by Corlett and Dumbleton; Cooper; Sutcliffe listed in references.
[5] FEFC Circular to LEAs, June 1992.

England and in Wales, to fund provision and to monitor the quality of the provision it funds through its inspectorate.[6] Under the Further and Higher Education Act, colleges of further education have a duty to provide courses funded under Schedule 2. Students with learning difficulties over compulsory school age have an explicit reference in Schedule 2, and are eligible for funding under the heading of 'courses in independent living and communication skills for students with learning difficulties.' They can also study other Schedule 2 courses open to all learners. However, evidence of progression must be demonstrated to other courses listed in Schedule 2, namely:

(a) courses leading to vocational qualifications
(b) GCSE or GCE A or AS level examination courses
(c) courses leading to entry to higher education
(d) courses preparing students for the courses listed above
(e) basic literacy in English
(f) courses in English for students where English is not the language spoken at home
(g) basic principles of mathematics
(h) courses listed under this section are the responsibility of the Welsh Funding Council and include proficiency in Welsh literacy.

While colleges have a **duty** to provide Schedule 2 courses, they also have a permissive **power** to provide other courses. The reverse is true for Local Education Authorities, who have a **duty** to provide adequate provision for all forms of non-Schedule 2 adult learning but also have the **power** to offer Schedule 2 provision. The responsibility for funding since the Act has been split according to what is being learned. For example, LEAs can bid via a college to run Schedule 2 courses with FEFC funding. Equally, an LEA may fund a college to provide courses in the non Schedule 2 area if they so wish. There has been great confusion about what counts as Schedule 2 and what does not: so much so that the

---

[6] Legislation and provision in Scotland was not covered by the Act and is not described in this report.

Further Education Development Agency (formerly the Further Education Unit) commissioned a project solely on the topic of Schedule 2 and non Schedule 2 in relation to provision for adults with learning difficulties and other disabilities.[7]

How was the research done?

The research was conducted in three distinct phases with different methods:

1.   Survey of Colleges and Local Education Authorities

A postal questionnaire was sent to established contacts in further education colleges and Local Education Authorities (LEAs). The questionnaire asked for information about changes which had occurred in provision for students with learning difficulties, and explored perceptions of the impact of these changes.

In total, 498 questionnaires were sent out to named individuals (365 to colleges and 133 to LEAs). NIACE already had a well-established database of contacts in LEAs and colleges. A letter which clearly explained the aims of the research accompanied the questionnaire. Chief Education Officers and College Principals also received letters, informing them about the research.

The postal survey was conducted between March and June 1995. In total, 280 questionnaires were returned: 215 from further education colleges and 65 from LEAs. This represents a response rate of 59 per cent of colleges and 56 per cent of LEAs (the actual number of LEAs contacted was 116: some received more than one questionnaire and others, such as Jersey and the Isle of Man, were not affected by the Further and Higher Education Act). The overall response rate was 58 per cent.

---

[7] Bulletin entitled: Educational Provision for Adults with Learning Difficulties and Disabilities, due out 1996.

2. Survey of Self Advocacy Groups

A student consultation group was set up to assist with obtaining the views of students with learning difficulties. Members of the group included students from a local college and a local People First (self advocacy) group.

In discussion with the group, it was decided that a very straightforward letter would be sent out to self advocacy groups. The letter asked them to send both good and bad stories about going to a college or adult education centre. This letter was sent on paper (with pictures) and on tape. Groups were asked to respond in whichever way they preferred (e.g. by writing, sending a tape or a diary of learning, or a drawing, painting, or by telephone).

A total of 70 letters with tapes were sent out to groups throughout England and Wales. Twelve groups responded, sending taped discussions, letters, drawings, or contacting us by telephone.

The student consultation group thought that it would be a good idea to talk to students directly at colleges and adult education centres, and made some suggestions about the sorts of questions which could be asked. This idea was therefore incorporated into the plan for the fieldwork visits, discussed below.

3. Fieldwork Visits

This phase of the study aimed to explore the factors that had enabled some areas to develop good or innovative practice. The criteria for good practice included evidence of collaboration, creative approaches to funding and work with a broad range of students with learning difficulties. The fieldwork also addressed concerns or difficulties arising from the Further and Higher Education Act which had been highlighted by the questionnaires. Accreditation, funding and exclusion of certain groups were major themes which were further explored in interviews.

13

Five further education colleges and four LEAs took part in the fieldwork visits. These sites were chosen from the returned questionnaires where respondents indicated a willingness to be approached in Phase 2 of the research. In selecting the colleges and LEAs the following criteria were used:

- evidence of increases/decreases in funding for students with learning difficulties and student numbers
- evidence of innovative practice/problematic situations
- geographical spread
- urban/rural mix
- size
- existence of minority ethnic population.

In-depth interviews were conducted with the individual members of staff who completed the original questionnaire. We also contacted any other relevant individuals suggested by respondents.

The in-depth interview concentrated on how the new legislation and funding mechanisms had been implemented, and the effects of the changes on funding for students with learning difficulties, student numbers, student support, type and quality of provision, and relationships between colleges, LEAs and other agencies. The postal questionnaire was used as a starting point: respondents were asked to expand on comments already made. Respondents were free to raise any other pertinent issues and were asked for further details on organisational structure, college/LEA policy on students with learning difficulties and any other factors which had influenced provision. Interviews were conducted face to face and were recorded via note-taking and tape-recording.

Interviews were also conducted with small groups of students with learning difficulties at each site, with the help of supporters where necessary. The discussion was based on a topic guide which had been drawn up in consultation with the student advisory group. This focused on the following points:

- getting to the college or adult education centre
- getting around at the college or adult education centre
- your courses
- choosing more courses
- getting help.

The respondents were also free to talk about any other issues which they felt were relevant. The discussions were recorded by tape and note-taking.

The fieldwork visits took place between June and October 1995. Interviews were conducted with 43 students with learning difficulties and twelve members of staff with responsibilities for students with learning difficulties.

How do the research methods relate to the text?

In order to help readers find their way around the text and to relate it to the methods, the following may be of help:

- quotations from adults with learning difficulties are presented in boxed sections
- quotations from interviews at site visits are described accordingly in the text
- other material, including tables, statistics and other quotes, derives from the postal questionnaire survey.

References

Corlett, S. and Dumbleton, P. (1992) 'The implications of the Further and Higher Education Act for students with disabilities in England, Wales and Scotland', *Educare*, 43, July, pp3–4.

Sutcliffe, J. (1990) *Adults with Learning Difficulties: Education for choice and empowerment*, NIACE/OU Press.

Sutcliffe, J. (1992) *Integration and Adults with Learning Difficulties*, NIACE.

Sutcliffe, J. (1993) 'The FHE Act and adults with learning difficulties and disabilities', *Adults Learning*, volume 4, number 5, pp132–133.

Sutcliffe, J. (1994) *Teaching Basic Skills to Adults with Learning Difficulties*, ALBSU.

Sutcliffe, J. (1996a) *Enabling Learning*, NIACE.

Sutcliffe, J. (1996b) *Towards Inclusion*, NIACE.

Sutcliffe, J. and Simons, K. (1993) *Self Advocacy and Adults with Learning Difficulties*, NIACE.

2:
Funding
and accreditation

This chapter describes the research findings in relation to four distinct areas:

* the overall funding picture in relation to adults with learning difficulties
* accreditation of courses for adults with learning difficulties
* concerns about funding and accreditation, which were expressed by one in three of all survey respondents
* positive aspects of funding and accreditation, which 12 per cent of all survey respondents highlighted.

With the split in responsibility for funding between the Further Education Funding Council and LEAS taking effect from April 1993, it was important to find out whether levels of funding had been affected and if so, how.

Funding has stayed the same or improved for most colleges and LEAs

The majority of respondents (83 per cent) in both LEAs and colleges noted that funding for provision for students with learning difficulties had either stayed the same or increased since the introduction of the Further and Higher Education Act. Amongst colleges, 65 per cent had experienced an increase compared with 42 per cent of LEAs. Over half of the colleges who recorded an increase in funding for this group of students thought that this was due to the funding methodology introduced by the Further Education Funding

Council (FEFC). The most commonly mentioned element of FEFC funding was the availability of additional support units (one quarter of those colleges noting an increase cited this as a factor). Other colleges thought that the matching of FEFC funding to individual needs had contributed to the overall financial increase.

Over one quarter of those colleges who had experienced funding increases for students with learning difficulties thought that this was because of a greater demand or an expansion of this provision. Other colleges thought that a greater awareness of the needs of students with learning difficulties (and an awareness that funding was available to meet these needs) had been a factor in their increased funding. As one respondent stated: 'The higher profile of students with learning difficulties within the Act has led to a more serious consideration of their needs.'

Amongst LEAs, these increases were mainly due to:

- successful applications for FEFC funding for Schedule 2 courses (e.g. through the Open College network or local college, or by introducing access courses)
- an expansion of LEA provision (because of the local authority's commitment to this area of work, or in response to local demand)
- active fund-raising from other sources (e.g. the European Social Fund).

A small number of LEAs noted that joint funding arrangements had contributed to the increase in funding for students with learning difficulties.

Around two in five LEA respondents (42 per cent) thought that funding for provision for students with learning difficulties had remained the same since the introduction of the 1992 Further and Higher Education Act. The corresponding figure for colleges was 17 per cent.

A wide variety of funding sources was being accessed

Respondents were receiving funding from a wide variety of organisations, as the table below shows. Three-quarters of LEAs received FEFC funding. The most important source of funding for colleges, other than the FEFC, was the LEA – 44 per cent of colleges mentioned this source. Not all LEA respondents (only 80 per cent) noted LEA funding for their provision. The overall use of joint funding was low (10 per cent of all respondents) but the proportion of LEA respondents using this source of funding was greater than amongst colleges (17 per cent vs seven per cent). A higher proportion of colleges than LEAs had obtained funding from TECs (39 per cent vs 14 per cent) and the European Community (36 per cent vs 20 per cent). Funding from other agencies (health, social services and voluntary organisations) was, however, more common amongst LEAs than amongst colleges (see Table 1 below for further details).

Organisation funding provision for students with learning difficulties	% Colleges (n = 215)	% LEAs (n = 65)	% All (n = 280)
Further Education Funding Council	97	75	92
Local Education Authority	44	80	51
Social Services Department	36	57	41
Health Authority/Trust	12	29	16
Voluntary Organisation	10	31	15
European Community	36	20	32
All Wales Strategy	3	3	3
Training & Enterprise Council	39	14	33
Joint Funding	7	17	10

Table 1: *Funding of provision for students with learning difficulties at the time of the survey (1995)*

A mixed economy was evident, with many and various funding bodies being approached to finance different pieces of provision. The following examples were drawn from site visit interviews:

> *One college has taken the approach that the FEFC is just one of a number of potential funders to ensure the broadest possible curriculum: 'I wanted to get as wide a basis of funding as possible – not to put all your eggs in one basket. Different organisations have different criteria and you can sometimes exploit that.' The college receives funding from the LEA, Social Services and the European Union as well as from the FEFC. The college has recently set up a two day a week course for students with profound and complex learning difficulties with LEA and Social Services backing. An employment project has strong links with Greece, whilst plans are also being developed for a three year professional theatre training course for people with learning difficulties.*

> *Another college has adopted a 'creative accounting' approach to funding. 'The Act has given us more flexibility ... If there's something I want to run – even if I have a whiff of an idea – then I can go for it partly by having different funding routes. I can apply to the LEA or go through Adult Basic Education and apply for Schedule 2. It's about saying "Yes, we could do that!" Playing the system imaginatively has preserved the provision: For example, a cookery course can now be called "cookery for independent living" and we can add on a very strong vocational bias ... and this can be funded through Schedule 2 ... We can now fund courses for people with learning difficulties that we couldn't fund before.'*

However, nearly one in ten areas have faced cuts

A slightly higher proportion of colleges than LEAs reported a decrease in funding (11 per cent versus eight per cent). For LEAs, the main factors in this decrease had been cuts in local authority budgets and the loss of adult education funding to colleges via the FEFC. The comments below from LEA co-ordinators who were interviewed reflect the scenario in many LEAs, which have faced savage cuts in overall budgets in recent years:

> *'The money we receive from the LEA has been cut year by year and so our ability to support properly is very limited ... we are all worse off. We've had the service cut over the past five years – it's probably lost between 40 and 50 per cent of the full-time people [staff] we had at that time.'*

> *'Over the past few years our budget has been cut substantially. We're not a statutory service, so if the council has to make cuts, it tends to be our budget that's been hit in the past.'*

The two main reasons given by colleges for a decrease in funding were that the FEFC only funded certain types of provision (i.e. Schedule 2 courses) or that previous LEA funding had been higher than current FEFC funding. A few colleges had failed to meet their recruitment targets and had therefore experienced cuts in funding. One college where staff were interviewed reported a loss of £100,000 worth of provision for adults with severe or profound and complex learning difficulties:

> *'We've provided for people with challenging behaviour, people who've lived in long-stay hospitals – and suddenly we had to make distinctions and it became clear that a lot of the things we were doing didn't actually fall within the FEFC remit. We've lost 350 places for adults with learning difficulties.'*

Although few respondents reported a drop in funding for students with learning difficulties, concerns were raised about the limitations placed on the type of provision which could be funded under the new system. Many of these concerns relate to the move towards accreditation.

One group of people with learning difficulties whose courses have been cut spoke up:

'I'm really upset about it.'

'I feel sad.'

'I did two courses and they've both been stopped. I liked getting out to meet people as well as doing the courses.'

'I want all the courses to keep going – I feel that I've definitely benefited since I've been doing them.'

'We can appreciate the problems the government have. But I feel that it's the disabled and old people – the less fortunate ones – who are suffering ... It's such a shame that they're losing out all the time.'

'There's another person ... at the moment he's just sitting at home because he can't go to the cookery class at all. He's in his 40s. All he does is go to a scheme and just sit in a room.' (This student, whose course was cut, has cerebral palsy and uses a wheelchair.)

'They need to give the college some more money.'

'We just want our courses back!'

Accreditation

Accreditation of learning has become increasingly important both to demonstrate progress and to satisfy FEFC requirements. There is a certain amount of data missing from the figures given below as some respondents were unable to provide any figures. It is not clear whether this was due to pressure of time or whether such data is not routinely held, which in itself raises questions. Nevertheless, the data gives an important snapshot of the scene.

Nearly half of students with learning difficulties were following accredited courses

In all, 80 per cent of respondents reported that, between them, some 27,500 students with learning difficulties were following courses with externally recognised accreditation. This is less than half of the total number of students with learning difficulties (58,000) reported by 87 per cent of respondents as being enrolled on their courses.

One in four colleges have no students with learning difficulties on unaccredited courses

Over one in four (27 per cent) of our college respondents said that there were no students with learning difficulties enrolled on unaccredited courses, compared with only five per cent of LEAs who said that this was the case. Just over half (57 per cent) of college respondents reported that students with learning difficulties were enrolled on unaccredited courses: 122 colleges had (between them) 11,529 students with learning difficulties enrolled on these courses, an average of about 95 students per college. The average figure for LEAs was much higher: 33 LEAs (51 per cent of our LEA sample) reported that (between them) 6,565 students with learning difficulties were enrolled on unaccredited provision – an average of 199 students per LEA.

Accreditation has increased, especially in colleges

Eighty-four per cent of colleges reported that the number of students with learning difficulties on courses with externally recognised accreditation had increased. For responding LEAs the figure was much lower. Only 45 per cent noted that this increase had taken place. Amongst colleges and LEAs, this increase was largely funding driven. Two-thirds of the college respondents who reported this increase stated that this development was as a result of Schedule 2 funding criteria. The same reason was given by over half of the LEAs reporting an increase in students with learning difficulties on accredited courses.

The availability of suitable accredited provision was given as a reason by one third of those college respondents and just over one quarter of those LEA respondents reporting an increase.

Although accreditation has become very important to providers and to the FEFC, what do people with learning difficulties make of it? The majority of people with learning difficulties are on very low incomes and many do not control their own money and finances. As one person said: *'I wasn't happy about paying £17 for a certificate from college.'* He had also had all of his work taken away from him, presumably to submit for accreditation. He planned to complain about this: *'They never gave me file back.'* [sic]

Concerns about accreditation and funding

There were a significant number of concerns about the impact of the new funding methodology and the drive to accreditation.

One in three people had concerns about funding methodology and Schedule 2 provision

Just over one third of all respondents raised concerns about the way in which continuing education for people with learning difficulties is funded and the resulting trends in provision. Although this was more noticeable amongst LEA respondents (50 per cent) than college respondents (just under one third), the concerns raised were broadly similar and are highlighted below.

Nearly half of the concerns raised related to the exclusion of certain groups from continuing education. Respondents thought that the emphasis on accreditation and certification was excluding students with severe or profound and complex learning difficulties. These students could not gain access to Schedule 2 provision if they were unable to demonstrate progression, as required by the funding methodology. This situation was exacerbated by the loss of non-Schedule 2 provision in some areas (due to a lack of funding from the FEFC for this type of provision, and cuts in LEA budgets).

One college governor subsequently reported that the FEFC apparently plans to fund only whole units rather than part or individual units of courses from 1996/7. He felt that this move could further marginalise adults with learning difficulties, who are more likely to gain part rather than all of a qualification, for example some units of a National Vocational Qualification rather than the whole.

One in three said that accreditation excludes vulnerable learners from education, particularly people with severe or profound and complex learning difficulties

This evidence was strongly reinforced by information from a different section of the questionnaire. Nearly one third of respondents (29 per cent) both in LEAs and in colleges, agreed that accreditation had excluded at least some students with learning difficulties from continuing education. The most frequently cited example of excluded students was that of students with profound/complex disabilities. Students in these areas who could not access Schedule 2 provision were faced with a complete absence of continuing education opportunities. One co-ordinator interviewed said:

> *'We used to provide quite good provision for people with profound and multiple learning difficulties. We have to say "no" to these people now – we can't say "hand on heart" that the provision for these people was working towards a vocational goal – which is what FEFC wants. Courses ... are not available for those people any more because they don't meet the entry requirements.'*

Another person interviewed commented:

> *'Colleges feel it's been particularly bad for students with least ability. And they are concerned, and I agree, that there is a strong possibility that people with multiple disabilities, who find it difficult to get into FE in the first place, may not then stay there. In some cases, however hard you try to play the accreditation game, they are not going to be a part of it.'*

Some people queried the relevance of accreditation across the board:

> *'Some students would have had their chances and self esteem improved through accreditation. They have now got the wherewithal to get jobs. So in this way accreditation has made a real difference to their quality of life. On the other hand, there is a cohort of students – like people from long-stay hospitals – who will probably not be looking at getting jobs, and so it's not going to make one iota of difference whether or not they've got a piece of paper.'*

There is also a training issue for staff in relation to accreditation: one area reports that some people 'aren't interested in accreditation – they are mystified and frightened by it.'

A two-tier system was emerging in some areas

Nearly one in five of the concerns raised were connected with the apparent development of a two-tier system and uncertainty about the definitions of Schedule 2 and non-Schedule 2. Respondents were unhappy to observe that

FEFC funding seemed to be geared towards more able students (i.e. those with moderate learning difficulties) in colleges, whilst the students with more profound difficulties were seen to be the responsibility of LEAs and Social Services departments. Two respondents reported that an FEFC inspector had actually told them that this was the case. Respondents thought that this development should be resisted, and that the divisions caused were not helpful to students, particularly where LEA funding was not secure.

Confusion about Schedule 2 and non-Schedule 2

Some respondents thought that there was a lack of clear guidance on the definition of Schedule 2 and non-Schedule 2. One person interviewed described the lack of clarity felt by many about what counts and what doesn't: 'There has been no guidance on non-Schedule 2. Some people will accredit a course and put it down as Schedule 2 and get FEFC funding and some won't. It's very much down to people's individual judgement. There's no real guidance.'

Another interviewee saw the difference between Schedule 2 and non-Schedule 2 as arbitrary: 'In some ways this is a bit of an artificial distinction, because they're all really doing the same things, which is teaching independence and autonomy.'

Provision for students with more severe/profound learning difficulties was viewed as a risk, since it was not altogether clear whether it would be funded by the FEFC. In some cases respondents noted that the risk was not being taken, and such provision was being cut.

Difficulty of demonstrating progression

Around one in six of the concerns reported by respondents dealt with the nature of the progression routes required by the FEFC. Respondents wanted to emphasise that small steps in a student's progression must be recognised, and that students may need longer to reach their goals than had originally been anticipated. In other words, respondents thought that the requirement for progression routes was only feasible if this progression was appropriate to the needs and abilities of students with learning difficulties. In some cases, progress was very difficult to quantify, in others, maintaining existing skills was in fact progress. The system needed to be flexible enough to incorporate these issues. A few respondents were also worried about what would happen to students who reached Foundation level, but for whom there was no suitable accredited provision to which they could progress beyond this point. The concern was that opportunities to remain in continuing education may be very limited for people with learning difficulties once they reach this point.

Narrowing of provision

About one in eight of the concerns which respondents discussed focused on a narrowing of provision. The loss of non-Schedule 2 provision and the emphasis on certification meant that choices for people with learning difficulties were becoming restricted, and the available provision was not necessarily appropriate to their needs. The emphasis of Schedule 2 on literacy, numeracy and skills for independence has diminished rather than broadened the curriculum. This topic is addressed more fully in Chapter 4.

Stress and bureaucracy

Implementing all of the new procedures in relation to funding and accreditation has caused headaches for staff, as the following comments reveal:

> *'It's created difficulties for us ... We've had to employ someone just to do record keeping for accreditation.'*

'I don't have time to organise other things now, as my day is so taken up with administration and dealing with Schedule 2.'

'It's been very expensive in terms of staff time to write our own submissions [for accreditation of courses]. You couldn't go and buy stuff off the shelf that meet the FEFC requirements. So people have had to write things. It's caused stress! It's taken so long.'

Danger of people with learning difficulties being seen as 'profitable'

Although it can be seen as very positive that people with learning difficulties can be funded to learn, there is also a flip side to this and a danger that people will see them as profitable:

'These students bring a hell of a lot of money into this college. And when you top-slice it, it pays for the Principal's salary or it pays for my salary, all those other things.'

Another person commented that there was an increasing risk of people with learning difficulties being seen 'with pounds signs on their heads'.

The funding system was not seen by some as being student-centred

The urge to secure funding means that many people are feeling compelled to 'go down the FEFC line', as it were: 'We've been forced along the accredited route by FEFC funding. We're overcoming it but we're not that happy,' said one interviewee. Two people summed up the feelings of many in saying:

'The funding is driving the provision instead of the other way round. So instead of saying what a person needs and then putting a programme together – instead of this, we're saying we have a course for these people, which is funded, so we'll

stick them in. Which doesn't seem to us to be the right way round.'

'It's helped us in some ways to focus in. But for some people we're quite sure that we're only doing accreditation with them so they don't lose their provision, which we think is wrong ... We're doing things with people for the wrong reasons.'

School link courses have been lost in some areas

The FEFC does not fund link courses with schools, which were traditionally offered as an integral part of college provision. Instead schools are now having to buy in their own courses. This has meant the end of well established link courses, which was mentioned by several people: 'We had to stop running the school link officially when we got FEFC funding.' Link courses provide a valuable introduction to college for school leavers with learning difficulties and an opportunity to see if a college course would be suitable as a route from leaving school. It also gives college staff a chance to get to know individuals and to help them settle in. It is of concern to many that automatic funding from the FE sector is no longer available, in some cases leaving schools to shop around for the cheapest alternative.

Independent living is not in itself an FEFC fundable goal

Although the aim of the majority of courses for people with learning difficulties is to help them achieve independence and autonomy, this is not recognised as a legitimate outcome in the funding methodology, which requires progress onto other courses. One person commented: 'I feel that independent living is a goal which is relevant to most people's needs. This is worthwhile and valuable and therefore should be a fundable goal.'

A sense of uncertainty about funding

Some people expressed serious anxiety about securing future funding to continue and to underpin their provision: 'We are going to have a full inspection ... we are fearful of losing funds.' Another person completed the survey questionnaire but decided not to send it in on the grounds that it could be misleading. Although the organisation had had a good year for funding, they were seriously worried about the next financial year.

Positive aspects of funding methodology and accreditation

A small proportion of respondents (16 per cent of colleges and eight per cent of LEAs) made positive comments about the funding and accreditation systems.

One quarter of these college respondents thought that the new funding arrangements had resulted in a higher profile for students with learning difficulties. The fact that they could be seen to attract money raised the status of provision for this group within the college. This had had a positive influence on the attitude of staff and management towards students with learning difficulties, and the needs of these students were being taken more seriously. Accreditation was also seen by some as bringing a much needed rigour to the work, as one interviewee described:

> *'Accreditation has made us focus and tighten and share that with the students. It gave us clearer guidelines as to what you're actually doing and working towards, and to finding evidence for this.'*

A few colleges said that they had managed to 'ring-fence' some funding or make joint arrangements with other agencies in order to safeguard provision for students with severe or profound learning difficulties.

Amongst these LEA respondents the main issue discussed was the potential benefit of progression routes for students with learning difficulties. This system recognised their achievements and provided opportunities for personal growth and inclusiveness within provision.

Similar comments were also made by several colleges, with the proviso that this system was only useful if students could show progression in the prescribed manner, or if the system allowed for slight progress to be recorded.

Benefits of accreditation for some learners

Around 10 per cent of those college respondents and about one fifth of those LEA respondents with increased numbers on accredited courses thought that this had happened because of the perceived benefits of accreditation. Respondents stated that accreditation helped progression, recognised achievement and increased self esteem. Two-thirds of the college respondents agreed with the statement that accreditation had helped at least some students with learning difficulties to participate in continuing education. Only 39 per cent of LEA respondents thought that this was the case.

Feedback from site visits

Some people were positive and enthusiastic about improved funding as a result of the FHE Act:

> *'It has been hugely to our advantage that the FEFC have put an emphasis on weightings – we are much better off.'*

> *'That's one good thing about the new funding. If you can identify a gap and make a clear case for the support you're putting in, it seems that they will accept that.'*

> *'Overall the support budget has increased dramatically, so it's made a big difference to the college and to my department.'*

Summary and discussion

The funding and accreditation picture is complex. The findings of the research highlight a great range of issues. Funding levels have risen or stayed the same for most people, although one in ten colleges and LEAs have faced cuts. The funding system is clearly working well for some people, who know how to 'work the system'. In some cases, this has meant being creative in retitling courses to fit Schedule 2 or in deliberately keeping a wide curriculum by looking beyond the FEFC for funding. One person who enthused about the new system also admitted to 'fudging' the funding to do things he felt were important.

Accreditation is easier for people with moderate learning difficulties to achieve and in the next chapter we will see how numbers of students with moderate learning difficulties have boomed.

Equally there are clearly losers in the funding and accreditation game, such as those with severe or profound and complex learning difficulties (who one in three people fear have lost out, or will do so) and the learners whose courses were cut completely.

3:
The learners

This chapter looks at the profile of who is learning and whether full- or part-time. It examines the details offered by respondents regarding students with learning difficulties attending provision both before and after the introduction of the FHE Act. Before looking at the statistics, here are the views of adults with learning difficulties on what they value about learning:

Learning skills and being treated as an adult

> 'I would advise college is a good thing to go to and the people there help you a lot. They help you with your skills.'

> 'Most people are nice to us at college: helpful, kind and treat us like adults.'

The social side of learning

> 'You could meet more nice friends.'

> 'Getting the company. And meet a lot of friends.'

> 'A very happy place. It's really good.'

A sense of belonging

> 'I enjoy learning things and I feel part of the college.'

> 'I miss it when there is no college.'

Student Enrolments

The scale of respondents' provision for people with learning difficulties in terms of the numbers of student enrolments at the time of the survey is summarised below.

No. of part-time students with learning difficulties (1995)	% LEAs (n = 65)	% Colleges (n = 215)	% All (n = 280)
0–50	11	31	27
51–200	33	47	44
201+	31	12	16
Information not available	25	10	13
TOTAL	100	100	100

Table 2: *Scale of provision in terms of numbers of part-time students with learning difficulties at the time of the survey (1995)*

No. of full-time students with learning difficulties (1995)	% LEAs (n = 65)	% Colleges (n = 215)	% All (n = 280)
0–50	67	47	52
51–200	3	38	30
201+	-	9	7
Information not available	30	6	11
TOTAL	100	100	100

Table 3: *Scale of provision in terms of numbers of full-time students with learning difficulties at the time of the survey (1995)*

Most LEA enrolments were part-time

Within the LEA group there are marked differences between full- and part-time enrolments. Two-thirds of LEAs had noted less than 50 full-time student enrolments (the majority of these actually had no such students) compared with 64 per cent of LEAs who had over 50 (and up to 1,000 in some cases) part-time student enrolments.

Part-time enrolments have stayed the same or increased in most colleges and LEAs

Around 80 per cent of both colleges and LEAs noted that part-time enrolments had either increased or stayed the same since the introduction of the Further and Higher Education Act. The proportion of LEAs reporting no change (37 per cent) was roughly similar to those reporting an increase (43 per cent). In colleges, the proportion reporting an increase was 59 per cent compared with 25 per cent who reported no change in these enrolments.

LEA and college respondents gave similar reasons for increases in the number of part-time students. These included the availability of increased funding, an expansion in provision, and greater demand for courses, in particular due to the resettlement of people with learning difficulties from institutions into the community. In addition, LEA respondents thought that their local authority's commitment to this area of work, and various Joint Planning initiatives, had influenced this increase. Colleges noted the availability of support and marketing of their position as factors which may have caused this increase.

Very few respondents noted a decrease in part-time enrolments (eight per cent of colleges and three per cent of LEAs). The decreases in part-time numbers noted by colleges were mainly due to loss of non-Schedule 2 provision and a decrease in funding.

Full-time enrolments

The college figures for changes in full-time enrolments were very similar to the part-time responses. Whereas full-time enrolments in colleges had increased, the figures for LEA full-time students had remained static. Amongst LEAs, there were very few full-time enrolments, and in the majority of responding LEAs these had remained at their pre-Further and Higher Education Act levels.

College respondents noted similar reasons for the increase in full-time students as they had given for increases in part-time numbers.

Most areas report expansion across all groups of adults with learning difficulties but at differing rates

With regard to the different groupings within the enrolments of students with learning difficulties (e.g. age, sex, etc.) a substantially higher percentage of respondents reported increases than reported decreases for each of these groups.

The statistics

The detailed figures for changes in student numbers are shown in Tables 4, 5 and 6 below. It should be borne in mind that many respondents did not answer some or all of these questions, either because the information was not available, or because there were no students in certain groups. Colleges were more likely to provide information than the LEAs: for most of the student groupings, 80–90 per cent of colleges were able to provide information on changes in numbers. The exceptions were for students aged 65 (where only 45 per cent of colleges provided information), students aged 45–64 and students with profound/complex learning difficulties (where only 67 per cent of colleges provided information). Amongst LEAs there was a much lower availability of information: between one third and two-thirds of respondents were able to respond to questions on changes in student numbers in different groups. At the lower extreme, only one third of LEAs could provide information for the 65+ age group, and two-fifths could give details for the 16–19 and 45–64 age groups.

Changes in numbers of students with learning difficulties in different groups since April 1993 % ALL RESPONDENTS IN BOTH COLLEGES AND LEAS (n = 280)					
Groups	Increased	Decreased	Stayed the Same	No response/ don't know/ no students	Total
Women	36	4	41	19	100
Men	40	5	37	18	100
Aged 16–19	44	4	26	26	100
Aged 20–24	40	3	32	25	100
Aged 25–44	36	6	30	28	100
Aged 45–64	22	7	33	38	100
Aged 65+	8	5	29	58	100
From a minority ethnic group	18	3	50	29	100
Physical/sensory disability as well as learning difficulties	48	2	33	17	100
Students with moderate learning difficulties	51	3	28	18	100
Students with severe learning difficulties	41	7	30	22	100
Students with profound/ complex learning difficulties	28	5	29	48	100
Students learning in integrated settings	60	3	20	17	100
Students learning in segregated settings	43	11	29	17	100

Table 4: *Proportion of all respondents reporting (at the time of the survey in 1995) changes in numbers of students with learning difficulties in certain groups since the introduction of the Further and Higher Education Act (in April 1993)*

Although increases were more common than decreases, there were marked differences between the different groups of students. For example, as the table above shows, the proportion of respondents reporting an increase of students in different age groups fell from 44 per cent to eight per cent as the age group rose from 16–19 years old to 65+ years old. Similarly, the proportion of respondents reporting an increase amongst students with moderate learning difficulties (51 per cent) was much higher than the corresponding figure for students with profound/complex disabilities (28 per cent). Hence the rate of expansion was much lower for older people and for people with profound and complex disabilities. This trend was more noticeable amongst colleges than amongst LEAs (see Tables 5 and 6 below).

Adults with learning difficulties talked about age as a perceived barrier to learning

> *'I'd like to go to night school to do a bit more work. I told my mum but she doesn't like it. She says I'm too old. I told her it doesn't matter what age you are.'*

> *'I know when they get to a certain age – about 24 – they can't go to college any more. A man I know was really cut up about it, because it was all he did.'*

One college which has opened up access for people with profound and complex learning difficulties described a success story during a site visit:

> *Howard, a student with 'profound disabilities' is on a full-time vocational skills course. The co-ordinator applied for additional funding to the FEFC and obtained £13,000 for support. He has one to one or two to one support throughout the day. In case of emergency, such as the car breaking down between sites when there is only one person with Mark, his support workers are equipped with mobile phones. The co-ordinator says: 'I feel it's a real precedent and I'm very excited about it.'*

Increased provision for people with moderate learning difficulties and increased integration in colleges

As shown in Table 5 below, 60 per cent of colleges report an increase of students with moderate learning difficulties, which is the biggest single increase in terms of student category. Sixty-nine per cent of colleges noted an increase in integrated learning.

Changes in numbers of students with learning difficulties in different groups since April 1993 % COLLEGES (n = 215)					
Groups	Increased	Decreased	Stayed the Same	No response/ don't know/ no students	Total
Women	38	5	44	13	100
Men	44	5	39	12	100
Aged 16–19	54	6	27	13	100
Aged 20–24	47	3	32	18	100
Aged 25–44	41	7	31	21	100
Aged 45–64	25	9	34	32	100
Aged 65+	8	6	31	55	100
From a minority ethnic group	21	3	55	21	100
Physical/sensory disability as well as learning difficulties	53	2	35	10	100
Students with moderate learning difficulties	60	3	28	9	100
Students with severe learning difficulties	47	8	32	13	100
Students with profound/ complex learning difficulties	31	6	30	33	100
Students learning in integrated settings	69	2	19	10	100
Students learning in segregated settings	48	12	29	11	100

Table 5: *Proportion of colleges reporting (at the time of the survey in 1995) changes in numbers of students with learning difficulties in certain groups since the introduction of the Further and Higher Education Act (in April 1993)*

Increased provision for people with physical/ sensory disability as well as learning difficulties in LEAs

Table 6 below shows that amongst LEAs, the group of students most frequently mentioned as having increased since the introduction of the Further and Higher Education Act was that of students with sensory and/or physical disabilities as well as learning difficulties (cited by 31 per cent of LEAs).

Changes in numbers of students with learning difficulties in different groups since April 1993 % COLLEGES (n = 215)					
Groups	Increased	Decreased	Stayed the Same	No response/ don't know/ no students	Total
Women	28	3	31	38	100
Men	26	3	32	39	100
Aged 16–19	12	-	26	62	100
Aged 20–24	19	3	32	46	100
Aged 25–44	20	3	26	51	100
Aged 45–64	14	2	28	56	100
Aged 65+	9	2	20	69	100
From a minority ethnic group	8	5	32	55	100
Physical/sensory disability as well as learning difficulties	31	2	28	39	100
Students with moderate learning difficulties	25	5	26	44	100
Students with severe learning difficulties	22	3	26	49	100
Students with profound/ complex learning difficulties	19	3	23	55	100
Students learning in integrated settings	28	6	23	43	100
Students learning in segregated settings	28	6	29	37	100

Table 6: *Proportion of LEAs reporting (at the time of the survey in 1995) changes in numbers of students with learning difficulties in certain groups since the introduction of the Further and Higher Education Act (in April 1993)*

Reasons given for increases in different groups

The main reasons given for increases across most groups by both LEA and colleges were the same as those given relating to increases in part-time students (i.e. an expansion in provision, greater demand and more funding available). College respondents mentioned, in addition, the availability of support for students with learning difficulties as a contributory factor, particularly for students learning in integrated settings. A policy of integration across the college had also encouraged growth in numbers in this group.

Other reasons for increases mentioned by both colleges and LEAs included better links with other agencies, Joint Planning initiatives, and the lack of other opportunities (for example due to closure of Social Services day centres or changes in Youth Training schemes).

A slight decrease in numbers in some areas

Although the figures are very low, the proportion of colleges noting a decrease in these groups shows signs of a similar trend: three per cent noted a decrease in students with moderate learning difficulties compared with eight per cent and six per cent noting decreases in numbers of students with severe learning difficulties and profound and complex disabilities respectively (see Table 5 above). Amongst colleges, the main reasons given for decreases in these two groups related to a loss of 'non-Schedule 2' provision (through lack of funding), an emphasis on vocational courses, and the need to show progression. These factors had resulted in decreased opportunities for students with severe learning difficulties or profound and complex disabilities. Hence student places have been lost.

The most frequently cited decrease amongst college respondents (mentioned by 12 per cent of colleges) was in the number of students with learning difficulties who are taught in segregated settings.

The reasons given for decreases tended to relate more to specific groups. Numbers of students with more severe or profound learning difficulties had decreased mainly due to a loss of non-Schedule 2 provision and the fact that these students were often not seen to be eligible for vocational courses or those where progression needed to be shown.

The number of respondents giving these details was very small, but they nonetheless reinforce the concerns already raised about the exclusion of this group of students, which were discussed in more depth in the preceding chapter.

Changes amongst different courses

Just over half of the LEA respondents and nearly three-quarters of college respondents thought that there had been changes in the numbers of students with learning difficulties attending certain types of provision, although only one third of all LEA and college respondents were able to specify these changes in any detail.

The main changes mentioned were similar in both groups – an increase in students on vocational/pre-vocational, foundation and basic skills courses (due to more money being available for Schedule 2 provision), an increase in numbers on integrated/mainstream courses (due to support now being available) and a decrease in non-vocational/non-Schedule 2 provision (due to a decrease or absence of funding for such courses).

Summary and discussion

Student numbers have remained the same or increased in most cases, which is good news. More opportunities are available for integrated learning, particularly in colleges. A remarkable 60 per cent of colleges have increased provision for people with moderate learning difficulties. However, despite the generally buoyant picture, there are some worrying undertones. Some student numbers have been cut, albeit in a minority of cases. Older adults and people with profound/ complex learning difficulties are starting to miss out, as provision for them is not growing as rapidly as it is for younger adults and those with moderate learning difficulties.

4:
Curriculum, integration and progression

This chapter looks at the range of subjects on offer for adults with learning difficulties and at changes which have occurred since the FHE Act was introduced, drawing on survey data. The complexity of establishing integrated learning and progression routes is then illustrated from site visit material. First, here are the words of one person about what learning has meant to her:

Self esteem through learning

One older woman studying basic skills has learnt to read and write at college, and has thrown off the stigma of being labelled 'mentally defective' in 1944/5. For her, education has changed the quality of her life and has given her confidence and self esteem: 'When I was younger, my mum had given up on me. She said I was mental. But now I've found out what is the matter, the whole world has opened up for me. I have really studied. I've put my whole mind to it. I'm really getting on well. Since I've been to college I really wish that my parents had been alive, so that they could have died loving me instead of wishing that I'd go to hell.'

The survey found that there was a heavy emphasis on basic skills ...

At the time of the survey, basic literacy and numeracy were the most common form of course for students with learning difficulties. Ninety per cent of colleges said that students with learning difficulties were enrolled on these courses at their college. The corresponding figure for LEAs was 68 per cent.

... and on independent living and communication skills

Eighty-three per cent of colleges were offering courses teaching independent living and communication skills. Two-thirds of LEAs had students enrolled on independent living and communication skills courses.

People with learning difficulties in self advocacy groups reported learning a wide range of subjects:

> *'We do photography, child care, food preparation and hygiene, computers, textiles and art, music and fitness.'*

> *'We like carpet bowls and squash and darts.'*

> *'I made some pottery and cakes and art and drawing.'*

> *'You could cook lamb, beef, potatoes and stuff like that and I did some work experience in the library there.'*

> *'I did literacy and computers.'*

However, not all learning was seen as constructive:

> *'We do stupid drama.'*

> *'Cleaning the cupboards out.'*

One person had been forced to learn about the body at college:

> *'I didn't want to do it. It was a load of rubbish.'*

And some people felt that there was little mixing with other students:

> *'We do not have the chance to mix with other students in the same class.'*

People had wide ranging hopes about what they would like to learn given the chance:

> *'I would like to do sword fencing and archery.'*

> *'I'd like to do dancing with men. I'd like to do happy dancing and cooking.'*

Vocational courses were more common in colleges

Amongst colleges, 88 per cent were offering vocational qualifications to adults with learning difficulties. Only one quarter of LEAs were offering courses leading to vocational qualifications.

Non-vocational courses were also on offer

These were offered by two-thirds of LEAs and by 47 per cent of colleges. Full details are shown in Table 7 below.

Type of course	% LEAs (n = 65)	% Colleges (n = 215)	% All (n = 280)
(a) Courses leading to vocational qualifications	26	88	74
(b) Courses leading to academic qualifications	11	46	38
(c) Higher education entry courses	6	25	20
(d) Preparatory courses for (a), (b) & (c) above	34	69	61
(e) Basic literacy/numeracy courses	68	89	85
(f) English as a second language courses	28	38	36
(g) Independent living & communication skills courses	65	83	79
(h) Non-vocational/non-Schedule 2 courses	66	47	51

Table 7: *Courses on which students with learning difficulties were enrolled at time of survey (1995)*

Changes in the curriculum

The majority of respondents (79 per cent) said that there had been changes in the curriculum offered to people with learning difficulties since the introduction of the Further and Higher Education Act in April 1993. This figure was higher amongst colleges (84 per cent) than amongst LEAs (66 per cent).

Switch to accredited learning to secure FEFC funding

Respondents were asked to give details of the main changes which had occurred. The most frequently mentioned change in these responses was the introduction of, or a greater emphasis placed on, accredited provision. Half of all colleges and one third of all LEAs made this observation. The most frequently cited reason for this development was in order to secure FEFC funding (cited by two-fifths of the colleges who mentioned accreditation and a quarter of the LEAs who raised this issue).

Growing importance of progression

One fifth of all colleges and 12 per cent of all LEAs stated that progression routes had been introduced or become more important. Again, the most commonly mentioned reason for this change was to meet criteria for FEFC funding. Progression is discussed in more detail later on in this chapter.

Expansion of certain areas of provision

Just over one third of all college respondents and one quarter of all LEA respondents thought that their provision for people with learning difficulties had expanded or improved since April 1993. In both groups the main factor in this expansion had been the availability of funding (including additional support units).

Amongst colleges, the most frequently noted expansion was in vocational provision (nearly two-fifths of those citing an increase or improvement). The need to attract funding was again noted as a reason for this trend. The main improvement in provision amongst colleges related to better access for people with learning difficulties to mainstream provision (one quarter of those mentioning an increase or improvement in provision). This was made possible by the availability of support via the funding mechanisms.

One quarter of the LEAs reporting an expansion/ improvement in provision said that their vocational or Schedule 2 courses had been increased.

Cuts in other areas

Twelve per cent of colleges and six per cent of LEAs thought that their provision for people with learning difficulties had been cut back since the introduction of the 1992 Further and Higher Education Act. The majority of college respondents in this group reported the loss of non-accredited/ non-vocational provision. Some respondents stated that they could no longer offer provision for students with severe or profound and complex learning difficulties.

Evidence from the site visits

Narrowing of the curriculum

There was evidence from the site visits to suggest that the curriculum was shrinking rather than expanding in some places. Courses were being set up with the FEFC funding criteria in mind, which therefore biased the curriculum range to Schedule 2:

> *'Increasingly pressure is put on the viability of running non-FEFC courses. Inevitably, the more provision you can put through Schedule 2, the more secure your funding becomes. We now get 43 per cent of our funding from FEFC, which is substantially more than it used to be.'*

One area used to offer a wide range of choices for adults with learning difficulties. Since the FHE Act was implemented, the curriculum has shifted and narrowed to be 50 per cent basic skills.

Courses have been lost

Interviewees listed the following courses as casualties:
> *Rural studies; music and communication; health choices and movement/spatial awareness for people with profound and complex learning difficulties; several arts and crafts groups.*

Keep fit; languages for holidays; introductory cookery courses, art. 'There isn't anything like a "holiday Spanish" any more. There used to be more of these, but they have gone now.'

One college lost a women's group, maths, cookery, independent skills and non-vocational courses. In particular, there has been a drop in the numbers of people with complex disabilities. One woman with complex disabilities used to benefit from social and community contact at college, according to her mother. Now she just stays at the nursing home where she is a resident and rarely goes out. Letters to both the local MP and to the FEFC have failed to change the situation. The FEFC view was that although it did not seem right, each college makes its own decision about how to allocate resources.

Quality of life issues

One college lecturer at a college which has had major cuts to provision for adults with learning difficulties says: 'If it [education] maintains the highest level of quality of life for those students then it's worth fighting for to the end. And I think they should be offered that as a right.'

Sometimes choices for students with learning difficulties were narrowed by availability of space in a class. One student said: 'I wanted to do computers but I didn't get on it. They had too many in there.'

An example of innovation in expanding the curriculum

One LEA was rare in reporting an expanded curriculum offer. 'A wider range of provision is offered now. We've found that over the last three years our source of referrals is increasing all the time. A lot of people were looking for a non-vocational type of provision.' The increase in referrals is attributed to the impact of community care: 'A lot of people are not looking for Social Services day care, so themselves and their workers are coming to us and asking what is available.' Courses have accordingly been set up in subjects to include music, computers, craft, cookery, health issues and drama. The co-ordinator says: 'People with learning difficulties are very keen to carry on with lifelong learning and to learn/acquire a skill for its own sake.'

Equal opportunities and the curriculum

Examples of positive discrimination in terms of equal opportunities and the curriculum offer for people with learning difficulties were very rare to the point of being almost non-existent. However, one LEA reported an innovative development in terms of a group for deaf adults with learning difficulties, taught by deaf tutors. Another college was working for the first time with students with profound and complex learning difficulties and also with people with challenging behaviour from a semi-secure unit. 'We can say, this is a place where all people learn, therefore all people can come. The funding of that might be fudged a bit. But if you think it costs £60 a week for 10 weeks, then that's nothing to a multi-million pound organisation. But the quality of life for those people might change significantly.'

Positive steps towards integration in one area

Integrated learning opens up the widest possible subject choice for people with learning difficulties. One area has an integration team based within the LEA and has found this to be very effective: 'Where we score is that this is our only job – it's not two hours tacked onto something else. It's well financed and well supported.'

But bad news for integration as well

However, the same scheme subsequently reported that they had been instructed by managers to set up Schedule 2 courses in order to expand provision with FEFC resources. The co-ordinators were worried that Schedule 2 criteria would limit the curriculum choice for students and that the move was also likely to introduce segregated provision, which was against the ethos of their scheme.

It is clear that the drastic cuts to general adult education budgets in recent years have undermined some integrated learning initiatives:

'We've lost people who'd become personally committed to integration. We've lost financial commitments to training people and getting them to understand the issues. We've also lost the ability to train part-time tutors, through loss of funding. We could dispel many of their fears and misconceptions in a day's training. And we could actually entice people to say "yes" to integration.'

'We probably don't do enough of supporting people into mainstream classes. But then the offer has decreased; classes are much more self financing.'

Some colleges also are setting up new segregated provision for people with learning difficulties. One college co-ordinator explained the increase in discrete courses for people with learning difficulties thus: 'I'm against segregated classes but because of FEFC it's dead easy to run those classes for two years as progression and as basic skills work.'

The perspective of colleagues from other agencies is also pertinent. As one Social Services day centre manager observed: 'We're no further forward on integration. There is still a separate "special needs" block.'

Progression

> One group of nine students with learning difficulties interviewed during a site visit for the project said that none of them had been asked what they would like to do after college.
>
> A student in another area said: 'Since I stopped college, I don't do anything now except go to the (day) centre.' There was no follow-up to her learning.

The topic of progression was frequently brought up by interviewees during site visits. Evidence of progression is required by the FEFC. 'I think it's been no bad thing to plant the idea of progression in people's heads ... but progression to categories that aren't appropriate isn't good either,' said one LEA co-ordinator.

Progression is seen as a difficult area by many

One college co-ordinator explained:

> *'It's always been a problem, since I've been in the service, for the last 25 years! ... People with learning difficulties, in general, don't show progress in the terms set out by the FEFC. Progress is slower for people with learning difficulties and they should really be offered much more time to show their development, i.e. not just over one year of three ten-week terms. This is something that has to be addressed if people with learning difficulties are to continue with FE courses, i.e. they can't just carry on because they enjoy doing a course for its own sake. Many people ... have nearly exhausted the range of courses open to them and may soon be in the position of not being entitled/able to undertake any further courses ... there seems to be just one chance for a bite at the cherry.'*

This contrasts with a college where there was no time limit on attendance at courses: 'If someone is genuinely learning and they are making progress at whatever level they are, then they should carry on.'

One college co-ordinator summed up the lack of progression in her area: 'Students were going round a merry-go-round of course to course and training programme to training programme without actually getting off at the end.'

However, one LEA service reported good links with local colleges: just the previous week 25 college leavers had been referred to the adult education service, which was clearly seen as a progression route.

> *'We try to avoid saying to large groups of students "That's it" because the reality is that there's very little else in the community for them. So we're looking at ways that we can offer something to students, but with a bit of progression built in.'* (LEA co-ordinator)

Limited opportunities to learn after college

The concept of lifelong learning is fine in principle but hard to arrange in reality given limited resources, as one college lecturer described in relation to progression: 'When they've finished a full-time course, it's what's going to happen to them after that. We've had one of the parents in this morning, worried about what's going to happen. If we can get them on one of a limited number of community courses which are about, then there's no transport – it's only for full-time courses.'

Adviser lost

One college co-ordinator said of progression: 'Before the Act there was a 16-plus [LEA] adviser who would help us with those sorts of things but now we have to do it on our own.'

Summary and discussion

The survey showed that basic skills was the most common subject on offer for adults with learning difficulties in colleges in 1995. Skills for independence and communication skills also figured very prominently. The FHE Act has had the effect of skewing the curriculum offer, as organisations have put on Schedule 2 courses to in order to secure their funding. This is a huge problem. Many adults with learning difficulties do not want or need to learn these skills, which reinforce the 'deficiency model' of learning.[8] NIACE has always advocated the widest possible curriculum offer for adults with learning difficulties.[9] The survey evidence demonstrates that the reverse is commonly happening: provision may be increasing in terms of volume but the **range** of learning opportunities is narrowing and shrinking down.

---

[8] See Sutcliffe, J. (1993) *Teaching Basic Skills to Adults with Learning Difficulties*, ALBSU.
[9] See Sutcliffe, J. (1990) *Adults with Learning Difficulties: Education for choice and empowerment*, OU Press/NIACE

5:
Support

This chapter looks at support for students before and after the FHE Act. Details are drawn from the quantitative survey, while students with learning difficulties also give their opinions. Finally it looks at issues of support for staff.

Increase in support

Most support services had increased since the implementation of the Further and Higher Education Act. This was true for both colleges and LEAs. The greatest improvement amongst colleges was in the provision of learning support and language/communication support. These were available at 71 and 62 per cent (respectively) of colleges before April 1992 and were available at 97 and 87 per cent of colleges at the time of the survey. Guidance and counselling was also available at almost all colleges (96 per cent) at the time of the survey. However, self advocates told us that sometimes professionals control who goes to college.

Who decides who goes to college?

People lacked control over whether they went to a class or not in many cases, with staff having the power to decide who goes and who does not, as the following comments show:

'I don't know why I am in this class. My social worker said I had to.'

'I was picked. Some people don't get picked.'

'We have to have interviews to get on the courses. We do not know how they discuss who does or does not get a place. It is disappointing when we don't get on the course.'

The least commonly available form of support in colleges was for self advocacy groups. Only 40 per cent of colleges currently offered this support. A number of self advocacy groups reported problems in combining self advocacy work and training with college life.

Conflict between self advocacy groups and colleges

Some self advocacy groups describe a conflict between wanting to go to college and wanting also to join in with self advocacy events, which has been seen as incompatible in some areas:

> *'They tell us we can't go to People First and college. Why not?'*

> *'Staff in college and social workers never ask if we have things like self advocacy groups, user councils or People First. They just put us on courses.'*

One area developed an **Agreement of Rights** to sort this problem out:

> *'Since People First started some of our members have had a lot of trouble with colleges and day centres to get time off for advocacy conferences and other advocacy meetings. They were sometimes told that they would lose their places at college or that they had to do their work at the day centres. A lot of our members wanted to play a bigger role in the self advocacy movement but were stopped by this ultimatum.'*

> *'We decided to take a tough stand to get our members' wishes heard and to give them something to turn to when in dispute with college staff and other establishments. We called it the Agreement of Rights ... It took us eight months of meetings and discussions with the staff and head of department at college before they signed the agreement.'*

AGREEMENT OF RIGHTS

Some of our members are experiencing difficulty in getting time off from college, day centres and other establishments to attend training events, conferences, county and local meetings and to undertake administrative duties involved with running People First.

We ask that our members be treated in the same way as are councillors, JPs, school governors, union delegates, etc. when we ask to be released to undertake self advocacy work, attend conferences and training, attend county self advocacy events and committee representation work, and for this work to be recognised and acknowledged as a vital community service.

We expect to be assisted and not prevented from undertaking this work and training.

Agreed with ....
(Name of service/ organisation)

and People First

Less support available in LEAs

Amongst LEAs, the availability of support services was generally less common than in colleges. The most commonly available services at the time of the survey were guidance and counselling (85 per cent of LEAs) and learning support (80 per cent of LEAs). The least commonly available were assistance with care needs (42 per cent) and mobility (48 per cent).

Full details can be found in Table 8 below.

Type of support	Available now (1995)		Available before April 1993	
	% LEAs (n = 65)	% Colleges (n = 215)	% LEAs (n = 65)	% Colleges (n = 215)
Guidance & counselling	85	96	80	85
Learning support	80	97	71	71
Support for self advocacy groups	49	40	39	32
Language/Communication support	51	87	51	62
Equipment	63	81	60	65
Accessible information	59	69	52	48
Accessible buildings	65	79	60	63
Assistance with mobility	48	74	51	51
Assistance with care needs	42	76	51	43
Transport	55	71	59	63

Table 8: *Type of support available for students with learning difficulties at the time of the survey (1995) and before the introduction of the Further and Higher Education Act in April 1993*

Access still needs improving

Around one in six of those respondents who reported that their buildings were now accessible, said that this accessibility was only partial or needed improving. This was the case for both colleges and LEA respondents.

Transport a major problem

Transport was also highlighted as a problem area. Cuts in Social Services/LEA budgets meant that transport was not always readily available, or if it was, colleges might be charged for it by LEAs. Some college respondents raised the issue of access to expensive or specialised equipment. This was causing difficulties, as the FEFC would not fund such expenditure. One respondent suggested setting up regional pools of specialist equipment.

One LEA co-ordinator interviewed reported that: 'The provision is there, but not the support to get from A to B. Transport can be set up, but if the centre doesn't have carer support, the student can't always get from the taxi to the class.' Office staff can sometimes help out on an ad hoc basis, but the co-ordinator says: 'I need resources to be able to support people more appropriately.'

One college lecturer interviewed said: 'They seem to be moving away from the idea of providing transport.' She pointed out that those students who receive mobility allowance don't always 'have their hands on it.'

Transport: complex and problematic

Transport arrangements for part time adult learners who have learning difficulties were complex. In one site visit interview with students, the means of transport were varied:

> *'I go by mountain bike. There's a safe place to leave it.'*

> *'I walk. It's not far.'*

> *'I get the bus.'*

> *'A lady picks me up from home. And then she takes me back to the centre. I get the bus back from the centre.'*

One woman who attended a different college until her courses were cut was also worried about transport. 'They're trying to cut the money for the taxi fares. People have to depend on taxis to go to the courses and day centres and now they're trying to cut this. Gail [a wheelchair user] said she'll not be able to go out at all.'

Transport problems

Problems with transport were a recurrent theme:

> *'The coach picked us up at 3 o'clock but our course finished at 2 o'clock. I didn't like waiting for an hour.'*

> *'I did complain about the buses being late ...'*

One person summed it up simply by saying: 'I haven't been to college. How would I get there?'

For some people, the size of a college was overwhelming. As one person said:

> *'When I used to go there, I used to get lost and I thought it was too big so that is why I left.'*

Dual problems of health and transport

> *One person faced a lack of support for his health problems from the local college. 'I was taking too many fits at the time ... so they just threw me out. I didn't feel very happy 'cos I just felt that I was no good.' He subsequently managed to join an adult education class only to have the transport arrangements break down after only two sessions. He reports: 'I seem to be getting worse with my maths seeing as I haven't been going to college.'*

Who delivered the support for students with learning difficulties?

Almost all colleges delivered their support through teaching staff and teaching assistants/learning support staff. Teaching and support staff were delivering support in most LEA provision (89 per cent and 66 per cent respectively). A higher proportion of LEAs than colleges reported that they also relied on other agencies for support (e.g. Social Services and voluntary organisations). Full details are shown in Table 9 below.

Type of support	% LEAs (n = 65)	% Colleges (n = 215)	% All (n = 280)
Teaching staff	89	98	96
Support staff/Teaching assistants	66	92	86
Volunteers	75	41	49
LEA	60	32	38
Social Services dept.	51	38	41
Voluntary organisation	42	16	22
Health Authority/Trust	26	23	24

Table 9: *Who delivered support for students with learning difficulties at the time of the survey (1995)?*

Around 90 per cent of respondents reported that (between them) some 2,500 support staff were working with students with learning difficulties. Nearly half of these were working on a temporary, part-time basis. Around one third had permanent, full-time contracts.

Support staff

For the majority of colleges (71 per cent), the number of support staff had increased since the introduction of the Further and Higher Education Act. The most commonly cited reason for this was the increase in student numbers and in funding. A further 24 per cent of colleges noted that there had been no change in support staff numbers. In LEAs only 32 per cent reported an increase in the support staff numbers (mainly due to increased funding), and 37 per cent reported no change. Very few respondents (three per cent) in either group said that there had been a decrease in support staff numbers.

Nearly half of all colleges and LEAs were using volunteers

Volunteers were used for support in 75 per cent of LEAs and 41 per cent of colleges, making an overall figure of 49 per cent.

Bullying and intimidation

Self advocates reported that bullying is a serious issue in colleges for people with learning difficulties:

> *'Pushed and called names and laughed at.'*

> *'I don't like the regional college. They call me names and swear at you.'*

Some people had been tripped up by other students: 'They stick their feet out in the way and that.'

Staring was also a problem: 'People look at you. They think you are from a different planet.'

> *'Other students give us looks and make faces at us. This makes us feel unhappy and uncomfortable.'*

One person had been bullied and staff did not help even when alerted: 'I would never go back again.'

One person even described having money stolen:

> *'Some of the students kept asking if they could borrow some money and they never gave it back the next week.'*

Health and safety issues

A number of self advocates were concerned about their physical safety at college:

> *'They haven't got a cord thing [in the toilet] and I would like one of them'.*

> *'Not all the college is easy to get to. I fell down because of a hole on a slope. Not everywhere has rails to help me.'*

> *'The car park is very dangerous ... too many cars and bikes there.'*

Learner support

Seventy-one per cent of college respondents said that there had been changes in the delivery of support for students with learning difficulties since the introduction of the Further and Higher Education Act, compared with 40 per cent of LEA respondents. Four-fifths of the responses from colleges where changes had taken place related to improvements in support delivery. Most respondents commented generally on the introduction or the expansion of learner support, for example the introduction of learning resource centres, the fact that support could now be linked to individual students, and the wider availability of support on mainstream courses. Others reported that extra staff had been employed (mainly learning support assistants). One college visited had done an evaluation of non-teaching staff. When support staff working with adults with learning difficulties were interviewed, 'it was realised how they were working well beyond their pay.' The situation was being reviewed.

Reasons for expansion of support

The most commonly mentioned reason for expansion or improvement in support was the availability of more money through the new funding arrangements. Other factors included an increase in student numbers, an expansion of provision, and a greater awareness of the needs of students with learning difficulties.

LEA support

Amongst LEAs, any expansion in support for students with learning difficulties was due to additional funding and commitment from the local authority to this area of work.

Support for accreditation: modified assessment on accredited courses

Respondents were asked to give details of any modifications which had been introduced in the assessment of work by students with learning difficulties. The most commonly mentioned aids to assessment were photos, video and audio tapes (mentioned by 39, 31 and 23 per cent of respondents respectively). Other modifications mentioned included the use of verbal answers allowing extra time, portfolios of work, practical assessments and 'individually appropriate assessments'.

Loss of certain support services for a few

A minority of LEA and college respondents referred to a decrease in support in their comments. These related mainly to a reduction in the ratio of support staff relative to the number of students with learning difficulties, and the loss of various county wide support services, such as speech and language therapy, which used to be provided by the LEA and were not funded by the FEFC.

Just eight per cent of LEAs rate their support as 'well developed'

Respondents were asked for their views on the adequacy of support available for students with learning difficulties enrolled at their college/in their LEA.

A greater proportion of LEAs thought that support available on their provision was under-developed (52 per cent). Only eight per cent thought that it was well-developed. Around one third thought that support available for students with learning difficulties was adequate.

The main concern amongst LEA respondents who thought that their support was underdeveloped related to a lack of funding. This was resulting in staffing cuts and greater reliance on volunteers. Even though there had been some improvements, more funding and staff were still needed if the delivery of support was to become at least adequate.

Some respondents said that their provision for people with profound or complex learning difficulties could not necessarily be adapted to meet FEFC criteria, and therefore was not eligible for funding for support. Other issues raised by these LEA respondents included the need for more planning and the need for staff development.

Only one in three colleges consider their support 'well developed'

Amongst colleges only one third thought that the available support was 'well-developed'. Similar proportions described their support as 'under-developed' and 'adequate'.

Amongst colleges who thought that their support was well developed, the reasons given for this situation included college and staff commitment, regular monitoring of support needs and ongoing training for all staff. There were, however, still concerns. Some of these respondents thought that more staff development and awareness-raising regarding the needs of people with learning difficulties was still needed. Other gaps identified were the need for more Joint Planning, the need for more equipment, and the need for more support for people with profound disabilities. One respondent was unsure about how much longer they could maintain well-developed support at the college.

College respondents who thought that their support was underdeveloped mainly commented on the need for more support staff, more funding and more staff development, including raising awareness about the needs of people with learning difficulties. There was evidence of optimism amongst this group of respondents: some people thought that current initiatives, such as strategic planning and the appointment of co-ordinators, would soon have a positive effect on the delivery of support.

Making information accessible

One LEA uses a mixture of informal guidance and a video presented in day centres to help adults with learning difficulties make informed choices:

> 'We've got a video of [names integration scheme] which we show new students. This year we had an "open surgery" where we plonked ourselves in day centres for a morning or an afternoon. And we encouraged students to put down their choices. A lot of students put down "computers" – and they don't necessarily mean they want to do a word processing or a computing course. So it's sitting down with them and finding out exactly what they mean by "computers".'

Making information accessible for people with learning
difficulties is important. Here are the views of a group
of students with learning difficulties on their local college
brochure:

'We don't like it. It's hard to concentrate on.'

'Too many words!'

*'It would be simpler to make it bigger and make the
wording clearer.'*

One student had been visited by a college lecturer at her
school: 'She had pieces of paper but no pictures.'

Teaching staff

On the basis of data provided by 90 per cent of all
respondents, it was calculated that some 4,600 teaching
staff were working in segregated settings with students
with learning difficulties. Nearly half of these teachers
were on temporary, part-time contracts. This was more
common amongst LEAs: two-thirds of staff had this form
of contract compared to two-fifths of college staff.

One third of all of the staff mentioned were full-time
permanent members of staff. This was less common
amongst LEAs: only 12 per cent of staff had this form of
contract, whereas more than two-fifths of the college staff
members were employed on this basis.

Almost half of the college respondents (49 per cent) said
that the number of teachers in segregated settings had
increased since the introduction of the Further and Higher
Education Act, compared with 25 per cent of LEA
respondents. The main reasons given by colleges for this
change were an increase in students with learning
difficulties attending this type of provision and an
expansion of the provision. There was insufficient data
from LEAs to analyse the reasons for the increase from
their point of view.

Very few respondents thought that numbers of these staff had decreased (seven per cent of colleges, nine per cent of LEAs). Numbers of these staff had remained at their pre-Further and Higher Education Act levels for half of the LEA respondents and 38 per cent of college respondents.

The trends for teachers working in integrated settings with people with learning difficulties was found to be fairly similar to those mentioned above. Since the introduction of the Further and Higher Education Act, 58 per cent of college respondents compared with 29 per cent of LEA respondents had witnessed an increase in these teaching staff. Again, a minority in both groups reported a decrease. Around one third of both groups had witnessed no change in numbers of these teachers.

Support for staff: information and training

As Table 10 below shows, information about the Further and Higher Education Act was mainly obtained through FEFC circulars. About two-thirds of respondents mentioned SKILL, NIACE, Further Education Unit (FEU) and the Department for Education as other sources of this information. The flow of FEFC circulars was seen by some as unpredictable. One college interviewee commented: 'I either get eight of them or I don't get any! You're never too sure when bulletins are coming out anyway and if they are not directly addressed to me, then I don't get them.'

Source of information	% LEAs (n = 65)	% Colleges (n = 215)	% All (n = 218)
FEFC circulars	91	96	95
Dept for Education circulars	66	61	63
SKILL	46	77	67
NIACE	75	64	70
Further Education Unit	55	71	68
College documents	26	57	50
LEA documents	49	34	37

Table 10: *Sources of information about the Further and Higher Education Act at the time of the survey (1995)*

Almost all college respondents (92 per cent) and two-thirds of LEA respondents said that at least some staff had received training on the needs of students with learning difficulties. In both groups only a minority said that such training was available for all staff (11 per cent of LEA respondents and 14 per cent of college respondents).

Respondents were asked to give details of any training on the needs of students with learning difficulties which had taken place. Only around half of those college respondents who noted such training were able to give any details. This was the case for only one third of the corresponding group of LEA respondents. In both groups the main courses mentioned were City and Guilds certificates, for example in Basic Skills (9282) and Learning Support (7321-01). The next most frequently mentioned training for both groups was in disability awareness/equality. Other training included specific skills such as Makaton and British Sign Language, accreditation and assessment for people with learning difficulties, and advocacy.

Amongst the respondents who reported the existence of training on the needs of students with learning difficulties but gave no details, the majority in both college and LEA groups specified that this training was taking place internally.

It is relevant to note at this point that a group is meeting with the specific remit of reviewing the whole area of national teacher training for staff working with adults with learning difficulties and/or disabilities in further and higher education. The Special Educational Needs Training Consortium (SENTC)[10] is producing a paper drawing attention to the need to develop a comprehensive framework for professional development in this work.

Training on the implications of the Further and Higher Education Act for students with learning difficulties was less common than the training discussed above. Seventy-one per cent of college respondents and 52 per cent of LEA respondents said that at least some staff had received training in this area. Again, only a minority of respondents (15 per cent of colleges and five per cent of LEAs) said that all staff had received such training. The majority of college and LEA respondents who reported that such training had taken place said that this was happening at external events such as workshops, seminars and conferences. Amongst colleges, the most frequently mentioned events were those organised by SKILL. Others mentioned seminars, courses and conferences run by the FEFC, the FEU, Cornwall College and the Staff College. LEA respondents mentioned the FEFC, NATFHE, FEU and NIACE.

In terms of the subject matter discussed on training events, the most frequently mentioned by both groups of respondents related to the financial aspects of the new arrangements brought in by the Further and Higher Education Act.

The following themes and comments from the site visits show that support for staff in key positions is vital. Many felt stressed and pressured.

---

[10]*Professional Development in a Changing Context* (1996) SENTC/Skill Further and Higher Education Monitoring Group. Copies available from Skill or from the University of Cambridge Institute of Education

Increased administration

There was a feeling that the FHE Act had brought in a lot of administration and bureaucracy which was stopping developments in some cases, as the following comment reveals:

> *'I don't have time to organise other things now, as my day is so taken up with administration and dealing with Schedule 2.'*

Awareness/understanding of learning difficulties by senior managers and teaching staff was often still limited

'There wasn't a great understanding of people with learning difficulties ... the Principal thought that a person with learning difficulties was someone who couldn't read very well.' The learning difficulties co-ordinator had to effectively educate the Principal, who was subsequently very supportive.

Another college reported that negative attitudes were hard to shift among teaching colleagues: 'There's an issue about teachers' values generally, about working with people with disabilities. There's still an element of prejudice. The fact there's no anti-discrimination legislation means there's real problems there. It's like we're being pushed out of the dark ages. We need much more disability awareness training.'

Supportive managers were seen as essential

People with supportive managers valued them enormously but were in some cases fearful of the possible effect of them leaving: 'I do worry that should our current Principal leave, then we might not be in such a fortunate position. I think a lot of our success has come through supportive management.'

The commitment was felt in terms of budget increases rather than purely in goodwill terms: 'Our head of centre is keen to encourage students to participate in the life of the centre and committed 10 per cent of the overall provision to learning difficulties provision. That will be higher now and they offer more provision.'

Low morale was evident in a number of places

There was a great deal of stress and uncertainty felt by many interviewees, as the following comments powerfully demonstrate:

> *'The changes have caused incredible frustration.'*

> *'The colleges are much more geared up to people having to achieve and to progress. It's much harder for **all** of us – students and tutors.'*

> *'It's a traumatic time for people going through it.'*

> *'From one year to the next, we don't know what's going on.'*

One college lecturer where provision for adults with learning difficulties has been slashed reported: 'We're fighting all the way.'

Summary and discussion

On one hand, support is booming and increased funding is being effectively accessed since the advent of the FHE Act. On the other hand, a pitifully low figure of one in three colleges and just eight per cent of LEAs deem their support to be 'well developed', which indicates that there is a long way to go before we get it right. Self advocates speak of the incredible frustration of transport problems and of the pain of being bullied and intimidated. Some staff too are undermined. The very high usage of volunteers raises questions about how they are being trained and supported for their role. This raises the question – what measures would improve these situations and how can support be effectively targeted?

6:
Liaison

This chapter looks at liaison between colleges, LEAs and other agencies and how it has been affected by the introduction of the FHE Act, which has substantively changed working relationships.

Contact between Colleges and LEAs

The majority of respondents (80 per cent of LEA and 86 per cent of college respondents) had some form of contact with other further education colleges. Amongst colleges, the two main forms of contact were through regional and local networks, including SKILL networks, and informal discussion with personal contacts through meeting at conferences or talking on the telephone. Around two-fifths of all college respondents were part of some sort of network and about a third of all college respondents mentioned their informal liaison with other colleges. There was also a certain amount of involvement in cross-agency planning groups/working parties/consortia, at which contacts with other colleges were maintained (about one in eight of all college respondents). A minority of college respondents mentioned specific visits to individual colleges in order to share ideas on provision or to take part in joint training/staff development.

For LEA respondents, the main form of contact with colleges was through local co-ordinating groups or planning groups (about one third of all LEA respondents). Informal contact was also mentioned by about one in five LEA respondents. For LEAs who contracted out some or all of their provision to colleges, the contact was largely to do with these contractual arrangements, including some monitoring of provision.

About two-thirds of both LEA and college respondents thought that the nature of their contact with (other) colleges had changed since the introduction of the Further and Higher Education Act.

A change for the worse reported by roughly four out of five colleges noting a difference

For many further education colleges, there had been a change for the worse, with negative comments outweighing positive ones by almost four to one. Colleges reported less co-operation and collaboration with other colleges since the introduction of the Further and Higher Education Act. There had been less sharing of expertise, materials, and information, and contact had become more guarded. This was mainly due to increased competition between colleges. Many colleges also commented on the loss of LEA-run initiatives such as cross-county training, county networks for learning support co-ordinators, and county-wide planning groups. These points were strongly reinforced by site visit interviews:

Liaison has been undermined

> 'Contact between colleges has clearly changed – liaison is worse. If someone from [names another local college] rings up to ask about something, then I'll say I'm unwilling to talk about that, which is crazy, isn't it! But there is now much more strategic secrecy ... that Act has changed the way we work.'

> One person was going clandestinely to liaison meetings: 'Ever since the LEA days, we established a co-ordinators' group – to talk together, work together, to do activities together. We still do the same sort of things. I don't think the college knows this

goes on – we do it despite them. I don't tell the Principal – I just go – otherwise it wouldn't happen. It's not encouraged at senior management level.'

'We used to meet and talk together ... now we just snarl and spit at each other and say "How many students have you got then?" '

Joint training initiatives have stopped

Before the FHE Act, one area had a county-wide approach to liaison and training, which has subsequently been lost. 'As soon as the colleges came under the FEFC, this stopped. The colleges refused to put any money in a pool to work across the colleges. We used to do a lot of internal training, which was good. This has now been lost as a direct result of the Act.'

'We used to meet regularly and do joint staff training. This stopped dead on incorporation.'

One county used to run a university-validated postgraduate training course, jointly planned and delivered by two local colleges in partnership with the LEA: 'We used to run training courses across the county. But those things have stopped now.'

Competition

' I think there's been a growth in the competitive attitude ...'

'I think what the split has created is a sense of competitiveness. You have to keep one eye on other providers and what they're doing all the time, whether you're encroaching on each other's territory. In our area it's under wraps, but every now and again it will erupt!'

Positive changes reported

The positive changes reported by about one in five of those noting a difference related mainly to the formation of new networks amongst colleges, although some respondents noted that this was less common with local colleges due to competition. Through these networks information regarding new ideas and good practice could be shared.

Changes from the perspective of LEAs

Amongst the LEA respondents who had experienced a change in relationships with colleges since April 1993, positive comments were on a similar scale to negative ones. On the positive side, improvements included more strategic planning, joint working, and development of new provision. On the negative side, respondents mentioned an increasing level of competitiveness leading to suspicion, hostility, or simply an unwillingness to provide information. In some cases, county-wide initiatives such as joint training/staff development and learning support co-ordinators' meetings had been lost after colleges came out of LEA control. The LEA's contact with colleges had therefore been reduced.

Contact with other agencies

Contact with other agencies (excluding colleges) was occurring for 89 per cent of LEA and 97 per cent of college respondents. The most frequently mentioned agency with which college respondents had contact was the Social Services department at the local authority (mentioned by two in five of all college respondents). Around one in five mentioned LEAs, health authorities/trusts or voluntary organisations. Other agencies included schools, Training and Enterprise Councils and careers offices.

The most common form of contact (cited by one in five college respondents) was via a multi-agency group, for example a forum for supported learning or college advisory committee on disability. A similar number indicated that there was also liaison regarding individual students, possibly at their reviews. Around one in seven of all college respondents said that they were involved in Joint Planning and kept in contact with other agencies in this way.

LEA respondents came most widely into contact with Social Services departments (reported by nearly one in three of this group). Other agencies cited included voluntary organisations, Training and Enterprise Councils and health authorities/trusts.

Joint Planning was the most common form of this contact with other agencies. About half of the LEA respondents reported this collaboration. Around one in five LEA respondents said that they were working in partnership with at least one of the agencies mentioned above.

Some change for the better

Changing relationships with other agencies were noted by half of the LEA and the college respondents. Relationships with other agencies were more likely to have improved than worsened. Respondents cited more frequent and closer contact as examples of this change.

For colleges where relationships with other agencies had changed, comments regarding improvements outnumbered negative comments by almost three to one. The main improvements were closer and more frequent liaison. Reasons for this included the need to negotiate funding for some provision, to develop provision according to the individuals' needs and to ensure achievement of joint objectives.

For LEA respondents experiencing a change in relationships with other agencies, positive comments outnumbered negative ones by five to one. The main themes raised by the positive comments related to an increased awareness of the need to work together, given the current funding position, to ensure that provision for students with learning difficulties was maintained. Respondents also mentioned an increase in Joint Planning.

On the negative side

On the negative side, financial issues were seen to be having a detrimental effect on relationships with outside agencies. Colleges wanting to charge for previously free provision (such as link provision) were meeting resistance, and in some cases, worse:

> *'Contact with Social Services (is) more acrimonious. (The) college wants a contribution for discrete classes run for their clients, Social Services refuse.'*

Financial issues were also having an effect in the opposite direction where colleges were having to buy in services which were previously free. The other main issue raised was a reduction of LEA contact since colleges became independent.

Negative comments from LEAs related to a general reduction in contact with other agencies. In one area, a good start after the introduction of the Further and Higher Education Act had since deteriorated:

> *'At first the Social Services department saw the Act as liberating resources for education for people with learning difficulties, but wariness of the progression definitions have dampened the original spate of contacts; local re-organisations to effect cuts have also had an effect.'*

There was considerable anger from Social Services and from parents in site visit areas where courses had been cut:

> *'Social Education Centres are quite cross that people who used to do courses are no longer able to do them. Social Services have found it hard to understand the way we are having to work. It's something that was imposed upon us, but it's creating a lot of friction between us and Social Services.'*

> *'Parents are very, very angry and very concerned. They've talked about the changes and they'd like this recorded. They're very angry that a lot of areas like cookery and music are being*

cut. They can't see a way out of it.'

One college was caught in the middle and had to build bridges: 'There has been a lot of anger from parents and carers ... the college has appeared to be the big baddie, cutting courses. So there's had to be a lot of bridge building. Anger has been voiced individually by parents and institutionally through Social Services day centres.'

One Social Services manager said that the local college was now only taking more able students: 'It's terrible now. People have to be literate and numerate to go to college now, rather than going to learn those things. They're just creaming people off.'

Joint Planning

Three-quarters of LEA respondents and two-thirds of college respondents were aware of their Local Authority Community Care plan objectives. Two-thirds of both LEA and college respondents were taking part in Joint Planning at a local level (for example working parties). Involvement in the formal process of Joint Planning was far lower, in particular amongst colleges: only 23 per cent of colleges compared with 39 per cent of LEA respondents reported this level of involvement.

Amongst both college and LEA respondents, 28 per cent thought that their involvement in Joint Planning had changed since the introduction of the Further and Higher Education Act. In both cases, the majority of these changes had been for the better, with closer and better communication. Not many respondents gave reasons for this change, but if they did, the mainreason given was the effect of the Community Care Act. Around a quarter of the college respondents who had witnessed a change said that involvement had decreased, mainly due to the loss of LEA initiatives, the lack of contact with the local authority, and the purchaser/provider split introduced into local authority services.

Just under half of both groups of respondents stated that students with learning difficulties had some involvement in Joint Planning, but the nature of this involvement was not specified.

Respondents were asked to cite examples of good practice regarding collaboration between colleges, LEAs and other agencies. They were also asked to mention any areas that were particularly problematic.

Only one in seven colleges responded to the request for examples of good practice or concerns regarding joint working. The majority of these responses were positive in nature. Most of the examples of good practice related to financial support from LEAs and other agencies which enabled colleges to continue offering non-Schedule 2 provision. Some colleges also mentioned the existence of good progression routes between community education provision and the college, or vice versa. The concerns raised related mainly to financial issues and the lack of multi-agency planning.

> *One site visit area had clarified relationships with Social Services: 'If we are offering a professional service to people, it's essential that we're not seen as a day service. We're not just somewhere to 'park' people for two hours. So it's very important that [Social Services] care managers come on board in this respect. The Act ... has kick-started us into going to care managers and insisting that care plans show there is a purpose for people in going to college.'*

Only about a third of LEAs responded to this request. As with the colleges, the majority of responses were positive in nature. One such response gave details of a drop-in centre for students with profound and complex learning difficulties. This was based at a local college, but other agencies were also involved, including therapists, community nurses and community education tutors. This LEA respondent also mentioned a 'taster' scheme being run in collaboration with Health and Social Services. Other respondents mentioned joint college/community education provision and joint working to accredit non-Schedule 2 provision.

Loss of strategic planning

The major concern raised was that there were no longer any overall strategic planning mechanisms. Local Education Authorities no longer had this role and the FEFC was not seen to be taking it on. There was no evidence from the survey that FEFC regional offices were playing a role in facilitating collaboration. Although some planning initiatives were taking place, these were by no means comprehensive. As a result, gaps and duplications were occurring.

> *One site visit area has seen the disintegration of collaboration, as the LEA officer explained: 'It was because the infra structure was disbanded. It went from a situation where there was a cohesive LEA planning unit with expertise to draw on and advisory services, to a situation where it's every man for himself. Colleges won't share what they do ... The overall coherence has gone. The planning has been totally ignored.'*

Local government re-organisation is a further complicating factor in the already fragmented scenario.

Summary and discussion

Half of all colleges and LEAs report better liaison, especially with external agencies such as Health and Social Services. However, for colleges in particular, there has been a steep decline in working together. Four out of five college respondents noting a change in working relationships say that things have got worse. Services for adults with learning difficulties have traditionally exhorted agencies to work closely together. However, the impact of the FHE Act in making colleges independent and competitive has completely undermined jointworking involving colleges co-operating. In some cases, the new college approaches introduced as a result of the Act have alienated parents and Social Services staff. The loss of strategic planning is another serious casualty. Without overall coherence, how can the patchwork of services make sense?

7:
Conclusion: a game of snakes and ladders?

People with learning difficulties have a mixed time at college, as the following contribution from one self advocacy group demonstrates:

We like:

- Getting certificates
- Friendly staff/people
- Wide choice of courses
- Good lunch food
- Improvements to the building
- Giving suggestions on courses
- Staff listening to our complaints and taking action

We dislike:

- Noisy refectory
- Verbal abuse
- Poor access
- Overcrowded rooms
- Poor transport

Just as there are good and bad things about college for this group of learners, so there are positive and negative aspects to the Further and Higher Education Act (1992) for people with learning difficulties.

Positive aspects or ladders

The FHE Act has undoubtedly achieved the following for adults with learning difficulties:

- funding has been put on a secure footing
  - 57 per cent of colleges have upped enrolments for people with learning difficulties
  - 65 per cent of colleges and 42 per cent of LEAs report an increase in funding

- opportunities have increased, for people with moderate learning difficulties in particular
  - 60 per cent of colleges report growth in the moderate learning difficulty sector

- funding has been freed up so that integrated learning can be more flexibly funded
  - 12 per cent of colleges report a decrease in segregated learning

- funding for support has increased
  - one in three colleges considered their support well developed

- a much-needed rigour has been introduced to this area of work

- the status of the work has been raised

Negative aspects or snakes

Equally, the FHE Act has had a number of detrimental effects, namely:

- the curriculum has been skewed to focus on literacy, numeracy and skills for independence

- opportunities for people with severe or profound/ complex learning difficulties have been cut

- one in three said that accreditation has excluded people with learning difficulties from continuing education

- liaison between colleges has been undermined

- support is still lacking
  - two-thirds of colleges thought support was only adequate or under-developed as opposedto well developed
  - 92 per cent of LEAs considered support was not well developed, of which 52 per cent said it was under-developed

- older learners are disadvantaged

- strategic planning has been lost

- bureaucracy and administration has increased

- some staff were experiencing low morale and frustration

- there is a danger that people with learning difficulties have become profitable, 'seen with pounds signs on their heads'

- funding has in some cases promoted segregation.

High hopes for the Tomlinson Committee

The Tomlinson Committee was set up by the Further Education Funding Council to produce a report and recommendations for the future of further education for people with learning difficulties and other disabilities. A number of people interviewed about the FHE Act and people with learning difficulties were looking to the Tomlinson Committee for solutions:

> *'The Tomlinson Committee is possibly our last hope. The goal should be to create opportunities for everyone to have access to the system.'* (LEA officer)

> *'I've got high hopes for the Tomlinson Committee. I hope these are not going to be dashed! I think they need to say learning difficulties provision is terrible. There's no guidance. What qualifications should staff have? What national training should we be doing? How can we improve quality in the classroom?'* (College co-ordinator)

> *'Tomlinson may be a good thing but it should have been done before the Act, not to repair things after.'* (LEA co-ordinator)

A summary of the *Still a Chance to Learn?* project was presented to the Tomlinson Committee. The Committee is making a set of recommendations to the FEFC in 1996, and these are eagerly awaited.

A game of snakes and ladders?

There are clearly aspects of the implementation of the FHE Act which have been very successful for people with learning difficulties. One co-ordinator who has seen provision develop and flourish in his college sees the FHE Act as 'a real tool and a weapon'. Whereas previously students with learning difficulties attracted the sympathy vote, now 'we've actually got rights and we've got the same rigour as every other course ...' The Act has led in the majority of cases to a growth in volume of education for adults with learning difficulties. This in itself is a major achievement, especially when the pre-Act picture was so patchy. Yet other effects of the FHE Act clearly give cause for concern, from skewing the curriculum to fit the Schedule 2 criteria to marginalising already vulnerable groups, such as those with profound and complex learning difficulties. There is still a huge agenda for development. There is a need to ensure a range of learning opportunities, with colleges and LEAs working together to provide the widest possible curriculum. Certain aspects of learning, including non-certificated education and quality of life issues, could usefully be allied to the Department for Education and Employment's recent focus on Lifetime Learning. The loss of overall planning and coherence evident from the *Still a Chance to Learn?* research means that a new planning framework is urgently required. This new structure should include colleges and LEAs working in collaboration with Health, Social Services, voluntary organisations, Training and Enterprise Councils and other relevant agencies. The results of the FHE Act for adults with learning difficulties could be compared to a game of snakes and ladders, with ups and downs and the inevitable winners and losers. The mixed impact of the FHE Act in practice was aptly summed up by oneperson interviewed on a site visit, who said: 'It's been a bit of a curate's egg in that there's been some good and some bad to it.'

An agenda for action

In conclusion, we propose the following five key recommendations based on the findings of the research.

- Adults with learning difficulties should have an entitlement to learn whether or not the education falls under the remit of Schedule 2 of the FHE Act. A broadly-based curriculum should be on offer.

- A new and effective joint planning framework is needed to plan coherent continuing education for adults with learning difficulties. The framework should include colleges and LEAs working in collaboration with Health, Social Services, voluntary organisations, Training and Enterprise Councils and other relevant agencies. It should also consult with and involve students with learning difficulties (and their citizen advocates where appropriate).

- The voices of students with learning difficulties in this report are mixed. The experiences of students and self advocates should inform future planning to ensure that continuing education is user-friendly for them. Ways of canvassing their views could include tapes, video and pictorial information.

- The funding and accreditation/qualification framework needs fine-tuning to avoid excluding certain groups of adults with learning difficulties from colleges, especially those with profound/complex learning difficulties.

- Transport remains a problem area which needs addressing creatively.

College would be perfect if ....

It wasn't so big
The other students spoke to me
I could do cookery there, but not make cakes

   (Poem by a woman with learning difficulties)
